Creative
WRITING
PROMPT FOR
KIDS

This Book
BELONG

TO

···

···

Creativity is intelligence having fun.

Can't use up creativity the more you use, the more you have

Being creative is not a hobby it is a way of life...

Being creative is not a hobby it is a way of life...

Creativity is intelligence having fun.

Can't use up creativity the more you use, the more you have

Being creative is not a hobby it is a way of life...

Creativity is intelligence having fun.

Can't use up creativity the more you use, the more you have

Being creative is not a hobby it is a way of life...

Creativity is intelligence having fun.

Can't use up creativity the more you use, the more you have

Being creative is not a hobby it is a way of life...

Creativity is intelligence having fun.

Can't use up creativity the more you use, the more you have

Being creative is not a hobby it is a way of life...

Being creative is not a hobby it is a way of life...

<table>
<tr><td>Name: ______________________</td><td>Date: ______________________</td></tr>
<tr><td>Section: ______________________</td><td>Score: ______________________</td></tr>
</table>

Creativity is intelligence having fun.

Can't use up creativity the more you use, the more you have

Being creative is not a hobby it is a way of life...

Creativity is intelligence having fun.

Can't use up creativity the more you use, the more you have

Being creative is not a hobby it is a way of life...

Creativity is intelligence having fun.

Can't use up creativity the more you use, the more you have

Being creative is not a hobby it is a way of life...

Being creative is not a hobby it is a way of life...

Creativity is intelligence having fun.

NAME: _______________________ DATE: _______________________

SECTION: _______________________ SCORE: _______________________

Can't use up creativity the more you use, the more you have

Being creative is not a hobby it is a way of life...

Creativity is intelligence having fun.

Can't use up creativity the more you use, the more you have

Being creative is not a hobby it is a way of life...

Creativity is intelligence having fun.

Can't use up creativity the more you use, the more you have

Being creative is not a hobby it is a way of life...

Creativity is intelligence having fun.

Can't use up creativity the more you use, the more you have

Being creative is not a hobby it is a way of life...

Creativity is intelligence having fun.

Can't use up creativity the more you use, the more you have

Being creative is not a hobby it is a way of life...

Creativity is intelligence having fun.

Can't use up creativity the more you use, the more you have

Being creative is not a hobby it is a way of life...

Creativity is intelligence having fun.

Can't use up creativity the more you use, the more you have

Being creative is not a hobby it is a way of life...

Creativity is intelligence having fun.

Can't use up creativity the more you use, the more you have

Being creative is not a hobby it is a way of life...

Creativity is intelligence having fun.

Can't use up creativity the more you use, the more you have

Being creative is not a hobby it is a way of life...

Creativity is intelligence having fun.

Can't use up creativity the more you use, the more you have

Being creative is not a hobby it is a way of life...

Creativity is intelligence having fun.

Can't use up creativity the more you use, the more you have

Being creative is not a hobby it is a way of life...

Creativity is intelligence having fun.

Can't use up creativity the more you use, the more you have

Being creative is not a hobby it is a way of life...

Creativity is intelligence having fun.

Can't use up creativity the more you use, the more you have

Being creative is not a hobby it is a way of life...

Name:

Date:

Section:

Score:

Creativity is intelligence having fun.

Can't use up creativity the more you use, the more you have

Being creative is not a hobby it is a way of life...

Creativity is intelligence having fun.

Can't use up creativity the more you use, the more you have

Being creative is not a hobby it is a way of life...

Name: _______________________   **Date:** _______________________

Section: _______________________   **Score:** _______________________

Creativity is intelligence having fun.

Can't use up creativity the more you use, the more you have

Being creative is not a hobby it is a way of life...

Creativity is intelligence having fun.

Can't use up creativity the more you use, the more you have

Being creative is not a hobby it is a way of life...